THE
LOOKING
GLASS

ISABELLA
GARDNER

THE LOOKING GLASS

NEW POEMS

THE UNIVERSITY OF CHICAGO PRESS

PHOENIX POETS

This book is also available in a hardbound edition from
THE UNIVERSITY OF CHICAGO PRESS

Library of Congress Catalog Card Number: 61-15932

THE UNIVERSITY OF CHICAGO PRESS, CHICAGO & LONDON
The University of Toronto Press, Toronto 5, Canada

© *1961 by The University of Chicago. Published 1961*
Second Impression 1965
Printed in the United States of America

For Rose Van Kirk
and Daniel Seymour

These poems first appeared in the following magazines:

The Atlantic Monthly
CANZONETTA
SUMMER REMEMBERED

Beloit Poetry Journal
SUMMERS AGO

Chicago Choice
A PART OF THE DARK

Chicago Review
SALOON SUITE
ZEI GESUND

Hudson Review
LETTER FROM SLOUGH POND

Minnesota Review
THE SEARCHLIGHT
A LOUD SONG MOTHER

Mutiny
LITTLE ROCK ARKANSAS 1957
IN MEMORY OF LEMUEL AYERS

Poetry
THE WIDOW'S YARD
AND THOU NO BREATH AT ALL

Prairie Schooner
MEA CULPA

The New Republic
THAT PRINCELING
MATHEMATICS OF ENCOUNTER

The New Yorker
AT A SUMMER HOTEL

Sewanee Review
NIGHTMARE
THE LOOKING GLASS

Texas Quarterly
WRITING POETRY
NOT AT ALL WHAT ONE IS USED TO

The translations from *Jean Sans Terre*, by Yvan Goll,
are reprinted by permission of the publisher, Thomas
Yuseloff, Publisher; copyright 1958 by Claire Goll.

CONTENTS

NIGHTMARE

A sleeping woman dreams she wakes
Into a surging room of shrieks
and shapes. In the frantic room a red
haired woman looms . . . on her bent arm
there sleeps a girl's carved wooden head
A doll-sized nursing bottle nipples her huge palm.
Both head and bottle drop and leeringly she
beckons. The dreamer screams her hatred
of the leering shape. Scrabbling for safety
the dreamer flounders on the floor.
The leerer pounces from behind the door.
The struggling dreamer stands
The dreamer lifts and clenches both her hands
The dreamer rips the red curls
in handfuls from that hateful head and hurls
the hairy gobbets at those manic eyes
The leerer dreadfully diminishes in size
She shrinks and shrinks into a little child.
The screaming dreamer beats the dwindling child.
The dreamer lifts a chair to smash that leering child.
Nothing at all remains. Not hag nor child.
No traces and no tokens.
The red-haired dreamer wakens.

THE WIDOW'S YARD

"Snails lead slow idyllic lives" . . .
The rose and the laurel leaves
in the raw young widow's yard
were littered with silver. Hard-
ly a leaf lacked the decimal scale
of the self of a snail. Frail
in friendship I observed with care
these creatures (meaning to spare
the widow's vulnerable eyes
the hurting pity in my gaze).

Snails, I said, are tender skinned.
Excess in nature . . . sun rain wind
are killers. To save themselves
snails shrink to shelter in their shells
where they wait safe and patient
until the elements are gent-
ler. And do they not have other foes?
the widow asked. Turtles crows
foxes rats, I replied, and canned
heat that picnickers aband-
on. Also parasites invade
their flesh and alien eggs are laid
inside their skins. Their mating
too is perilous. The meeting
turns their faces blue with bliss
and consummation of this
absolute embrace is so
extravagantly slow
in coming that love begun
at dawn may end in fatal sun.

The widow told me that her
husband knew snails' ways and his garden had been Eden for them. He
said the timid snail could lift three
times his weight straight up and haul
a wagon toy loaded with a whole
two hundred times his body's burden.
Then as we left the garden
she said that at the first faint chill
the first premonition of fall
the snails go straight to earth . . . excrete
the lime with which they then secrete
the opening in their shells . . . and wait for spring.
It is those little doors which sing,
she said, when they are boiled.
She smiled at me when I recoiled.

ZEI GESUND*

For Dr. Louis Cholden
1918–1956

In the preposterous sunlight
we watched them wincingly lower you
into your formal April grave.
In strict tears they tolled the Hebrew
litanies which (though you were not pious)
had wailed in the ark of your ear
and blown in the shule of your heart
as remindingly as Shofar.
You lived your life and died your death by
love, and if on that spring day you could
have spoken from the upholstered
isolation of your coffin, you would
have taken to yourself the sorrow
of your uncountable bereaved,
as you did always, possibly saying "that
I am the reason you are grieved
and that I cannot rouse to laugh you out
of tears distresses me as dying
can no longer." Louis, it is true
that when those loved do die our crying
is made most difficult to suffer
by the unstoppable sharing
of what we imagine to have been
the die-er's panic and despairing
in this ultimate encounter.
You spared us that pain, for knowing
your life-spirit robust past compare
we knew that you had braved your going
with your accustomed curiosity

---

* *Zei Gesund* is a Yiddish phrase meaning literally "Be well"; it is used in leave-taking; therefore: "Farewell." *Shule* is the Jewish word for temple; *shofar*, for the ram's horn blown on the Day of Judgment.

and calm and courage. Every tear
is for ourselves, for our own loss,
the forever absence of you. Were
Death a hag (like those dishevelled
ladies in asylums whom you re-
deemed to dignity through your
accepting word and touch) I do be-
lieve you would have lent Ma Death a
comb for her lank locks and would fear-
lessly have stroked her fleshless shoulder
saying gently "Why Mrs. Bones, my dear,
haven't you come a little early?"
I think you would not have withheld
even from Death's self your thou-ing
greeting once you beheld
that incurable at your elbow.
You fought to keep her waiting for
you in the hallway while she
scratched and finally pounded on your door
but once she entered and that door closed
behind her you recognized the fact
of her outrageous presence and the
courtesy and courage of your heart listened intact
to her untimely undeniable demand.

It is not easy to remember that you died.
Neither your funeral nor our tears persuade
us, yet, that you have died. We shall confide
to you in phantasy through years of need
the flabby failure, shabby sin, and pride-
fully, the high Hungarian deed.
Our spirits shall by your quick soul be fed
until our bodies, too, are dead.

IN MEMORY OF LEMUEL AYERS, SCENE DESIGNER,
Dead of Cancer in His Fortieth Year.

It is generall
To be mortall
I have well espied
No man may him hide
from death hollow-eyed.

John Skelton

I that indulgently
am still allowed to be
address these lines to the
"Late Lemuel Ayers" who
did not elect to do
his dying young

Lem you are early late
your life and death complete,
somewhere our dyings wait.
Finished with and by pain
you will not feel again
forgive us grief

Magical from the start
your strict and dazzling art
pure as your eye's taut heart
delicate bold and rare
castled the empty air
splendoring space

Truth-vizored knight of risk
vulnerable in your casque
magician of the masque
sword-wand in hand you strove
to conquer goat-foot's grove,
laurel your crown

Raped of felicity
ambushed unknowingly
by your bones' treachery
outraged by cone and knife
you labored for your life,
Myrtle, your wreath

Now you indulgently
observe our boon to be
alive and grieved, but the
shame is you've few friends who
dare to expect to do
their dying old.

ON LOOKING IN THE LOOKING GLASS

Your small embattled eyes dispute a face
that middle-aging sags and creases.
Besieged, your eyes protest and plead,
your wild little eyes are bright, and bleed.

And now in an instant's blink my stare
seizes in your beleaguered glare
the pristine gaze the blown-glass stance
of your once
total innocence.
I see and dare the child you were.

And for a wink's lasting, There
Now in your blistered eyes dazzles the flare
of Youth with years and love to swear
the kindling enkindled fire
heedless and sheer . . .
I see and fear the girl you were.

And now for a tic's lending, Now for the stint
of a second's fission I light to the glint
of your Daemon, that familiar whom you stint
so prodigally. Shunting, shan't-
ing, wincing fabricant
I see the maker that you want
and aren't.

And now just now I closed your eyes
your infant ancient naked eyes.
Gaze glare and flare and glint are buried by
my neutral eye-
lids. These island citadels are now surrendered
and with imagination's eye I see you dead.

".... AND THOU NO BREATH AT ALL?"

for Barbara Ransom Jopson, 1915–1957

Yours, Barbara, was a literal way of death.
You were defaulted by the failure of your breath.
To fox the taxing of your faltering breath
you schooled yourself for years to snare
a reasonable surety of air . . .
not surplus air to waltz or to embrace
just marginal sips to stay, with grace,
alight, and spark the hovering dark of death
with bright unwavering speech. You flogged your breath
down your dogged days and spent that wilting breath
in dialogues that burnished us with your
ungarnishable gold where we before
had counterfeited in our brass or gilt. Your art
was alchemy wrought by a sleight of heart.
That art will lend us gold beyond your death
and round the bend of our last breath
when we like you end, as we must, all out of breath.

SALOON SUITE

I. *Accordion and Harmonica*

(Accordion)   *Waltz*

The red balloon will collapse, my sweet
The snowman will melt in the sun
The daffodil dries on the hill
                     AND
the kite blows away out of sight
But the hurdy the gurdy still giddies the street
                and lilacs are BLOO-
                   ming in Kew
and the dancing   the dancing
the rhyming romancing
will never no never be done.

(Harmonica)   *Jig*

Murphy and company jig with Cohen
Shicker vie a Goy
Sing your slainthe landsmen
Lhude sing Lochheim
Joy and joy and joy
AND
Paesani   Please   It's time

NOTE.—This poem was written after hearing the "Third Man Theme," which should be kept in mind while reading Part II. "Shicker vie a Goy" is Yiddish for "drunk like a gentile," "Slainthe" is the Gaelic equivalent of "Here's to you," and "Lochheim" is Yiddish for "slainthe." "Landsmen" is Yiddish for "fellow townsmen."

SALOON SUITE

II. *Zither*   *Tango*

Loving you Love loving you
the least leaf
the least last lone-est leaf
redder is, red red is redder
redder than that maple grove
in fall   in fall in fall
                              and in
and in the spring in the spring
the youngest and the littlest leaf
                    is green
a greener green a greenest green ah greener than
a willow tree
                    in May
in May in May
I love you, love you love you far-
ther, than the farthest foam in
furthest most for ever wake of sea-
lost shallop
and more particularly Love, than
the look! look looked-for shell than
the sought-found-shell than
the small and the whole shell's
sweet scallop.
Lost love-lost love-lost
I am lost Love I am lost love-lost
Love lost.
Sail me sail me home
Sail me sail me sail me home
My sailor sail me sail me home
Reef me steer me. Navigate me
home   home home home
home.

LITTLE ROCK ARKANSAS 1957

dedicated to the nine children

Clasping like bucklers to their bodies, books,
nine children move through blasts of killing looks.
Committed to this battle each child dares,
deliberately, the fusillades of jeers.
Their valor iron in their ironed clothes
they walk politely in their polished shoes
down ambushed halls to classrooms sown with mines
to learn their lesson. Obviously nine's
a carefully calculated number, odd
not even, a suave size that can be add-
ed to, discreetly, later, or culled now
should one child break not bend; or fail to bow
sufficiently his bloody head . . . a rule
to heed, child, be you black and going to school.

LETTER FROM SLOUGH POND

Here where you left me alone
the soft wind sighs through my wishbone
the sun is lapping at my flesh
I couple with the ripples of the fresh
pond water I am rolled by the roiling sea.
Love, in our wide bed, do you lie lonely?
The spoon of longing stirs my marrow
and I thank God this bed is narrow.

MATHEMATICS OF ENCOUNTER

Two never-ever-will-be lovers each
thatched in a thicket of one-
liness, huddled in onlyhood,
reach eye to perilous eye and contract
in an absolute gaze, in a clasping
of I's, a wedding. In that (ah marginal)
marrying of marrows, flesh blooms and bells,
blood shimmers and arrows, bones melt
and meld, loins lock.
In that look's-lasting love is resolved
to one-plus-one, dissolved again to two, these
    two absolved,
and the equation solved.

MEA CULPA

I do not love thee, Doctor Fell
The reason why I cannot tell
But this one thing I know full well
I do not love thee, Dr. Fell

The plane rose loudly and rammed west
while I, as usual afraid, rejoiced
that the stranger beside me hid
the window's terrible view of our toy
enormous tinkered wing tilting
and shuddering out there
in the middle of the air.

I looked at the man by my side
and saw one eye, cheek, ear, and hearing aid.
His tears fell out the eye and down the cheek.
Turning his head he fused his spilling gaze
to mine and begging angrily he said
"I am a surgeon hired to patch
the almost dead alive
but Doctor Fell will not arrive.

He is expected; and further
he is expected by the families
of the dying, who pay his monstrous fee
and fare, to be God Almighty's cousin . . .
whereas, clearly, I am not even
on time, lady, not even perhaps in
time, because a flight was cancelled." Knowing
him deaf I loudly cried
him grace, yelling, "You tried . . .
and they will know that you tried."

28

He mentioned trains and that they run on time
and that perhaps the waiting dying man
had died. "Yes, I am a surgeon," he said
softly, "but I had rather peddle used
cars to buy my beer. I am tired I
am tired of this frightful trust when I
confront and cut a bleeding carcass."
Touching his hand I blared
that the very FACT that he cared . . .

"Care, care," he said as tears still slid
from his eyes, "can't you see I am not there?"
Abruptly he pulled a silver pill-box
from his pocket, and showing me his hands
and how they shook, he said, "I take a pill
at intervals to make my hands belong
and if I time the taking perfectly
these hands behave; they are golden, lady,
not one qualm or quiver in these
fingers, in these wrists, this heart,
or any other part."

I thought but could not bellow, yes, you care,
but the choice was yours; you made it leniently.
Your tears and pills and knives, my glib compassion
and my cadenced cant, these bleeding hearts
that blossom on our sleeves will not enlarge the
spirit, Doctor, nor reduce the spleen. We
must commit the act of caring before
indulging in elegiac tears. Our bills and
visits must be paid, our letters written,
our departures and arrivals made on time.
Trusting your weather eye
you assumed that plane would fly.

"Please forgive me that I have no comfort
for you".... I spoke out loud, but, not, it seemed,
quite loud enough, for he paid no heed, and
kneading his hands, remained silent until
our plane landed. I wished then to will him
well, but under the circumstances,
a resonant Good Luck struck me as flippant,
and a shouted Good-bye redundant.